My Mum the Crazy Chicken Lady

My Mum the Crazy Chicken Lady

Eliza Hutchinson

Dedicated to my Mum and dad for always teaching me to be strong and brave and let my uniqueness sparkle

"Live a little love a lot "
Kenny Chesney

{ 1 }

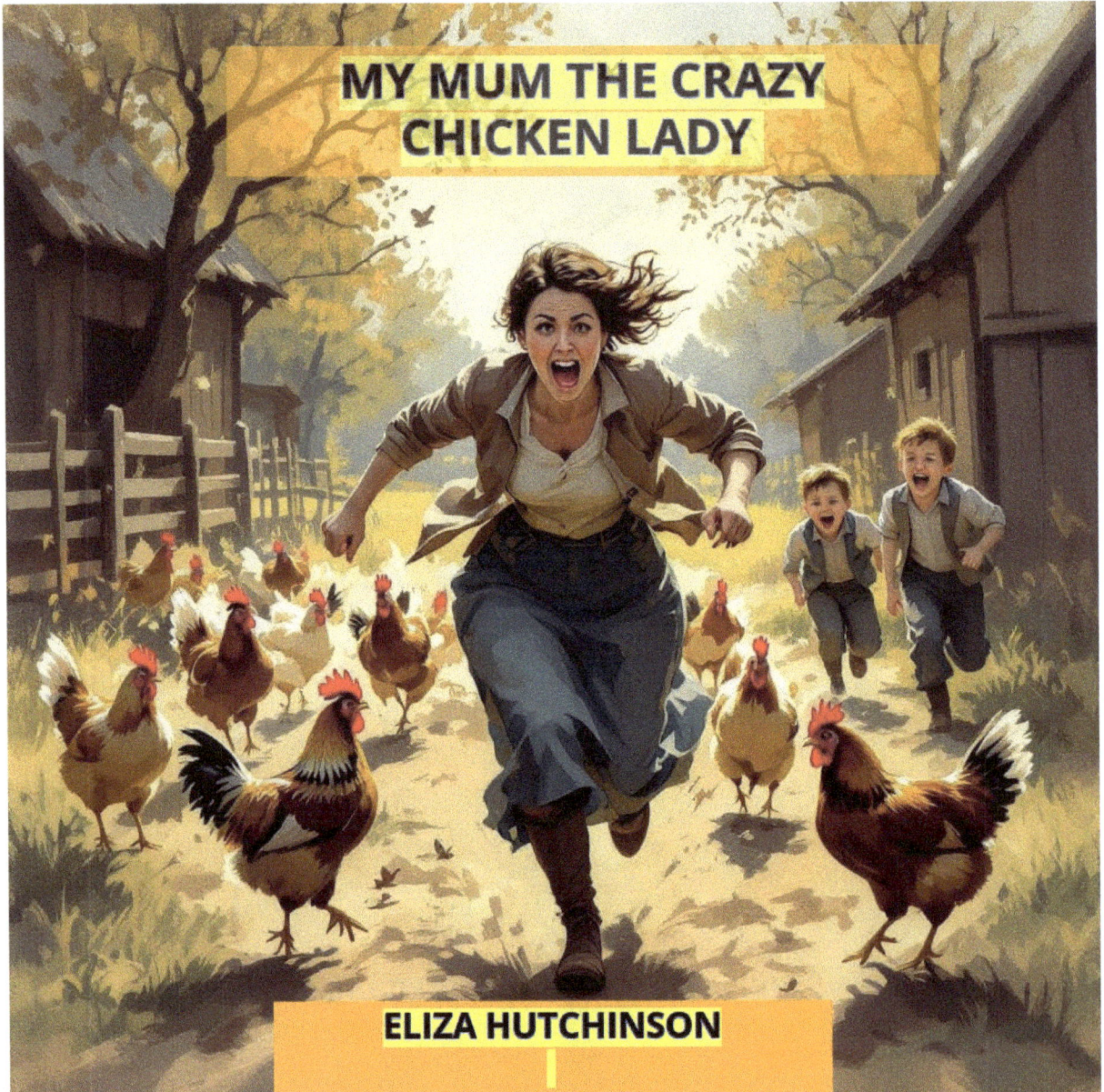

MY MUM THE CRAZY CHICKEN LADY

ELIZA HUTCHINSON

{ 2 }

{ **3** }

Cover Design: Eliza Hutchinson
Illustrations: AI-assisted, edited by the author
Published by: Independently Published
ISBN: 9780646731148

Eliza Hutchinson is a children's author and a dedicated nurse. When she isn't writing whimsical stories for young readers, Eliza can be found in her garden surrounded by her much-loved chickens, enjoying time with her family, or heading out on new adventures. She has a deep love for books, and in her spare time she enjoys reading and creating new stories that inspire imagination and curiosity

I would like to extend my deepest gratitude to my entire family for your endless love, support, and belief in me. Your encouragement has carried me through every step of this journey. Thank you for reminding me to keep going, to dream boldly, and to trust in myself. This book is as much yours as it is mine.

My mummy loves her chickens —
Big, medium, and small,
Red and black, white and gold,
She really loves them

She's happiest in the garden,
With scraps and seeds to share,
Beetles, veggies, tasty bits —
She gives them all with care.

When we go out shopping,
She's not buying things for us,
She's looking at chicken coops and feed,
Without much fuss or rush.

She's got twelve fluffy chickens —
But still wants one or two more.
I say, "Isn't that enough?"
She laughs and heads back to the store.
When she's mad or feeling grumpy,
She hugs her girls so tight,
They squawk and flap and try to run,
But it makes her feel alright.

They run up to the fence each day,
Excited for their treats,
And mummy smiles, her heart so full,
As she pours out all their food.
She builds them homes like little towns,
Painted green and blue and bright,
With room to roam and scratch and play,
From morning until night.

She searches for their eggs each day,
In bushes, trees, and coops,
Sometimes she drops them on her shoes —
Right into chicken poops!

She loves the eggs in colours bright —
Red, white, and even blue,
She takes a photo every time
And bakes sweet treats for you.

She talks to all her chickens,
Like they're her closest friends,
"They're good at keeping secrets,"
She says, "And loyal to the end."

When they escape, she runs around
With feathers flying past,
She huffs and puffs and stomps her feet,
But still she has a blast.

She doesn't mind the mess they make,
Or cleaning up their poo,
She laughs and says, "It's all worth it —
It's what crazy chicken mums do!"

But best of all, she beams with joy
When we come help or play,
And when we tease, she grins and says:
"I need my chickens — and you — to stay sane every day."

The END

BLURB

In the charming and funny tale, Mum juggles feathers and family as she tends to her cheeky chickens and keeps up with her adventurous sons. Whether she's rescuing wayward hens, sharing magical backyard stories, or giving the warmest cuddles a kid could ask for, Mum proves that love comes in all shapes, sizes, and sometimes... with feathers.

A joyful celebration of motherhood, family, and the bond between kids and their story reminds us that and a whole lot of clucking.

www.ingramcontent.com/pod-product-compliance
Lightning Source LLC
Chambersburg PA
CBHW062008090426
42811CB00005B/783